Wings

of a

Dove

Inspired by God

Written By:

Amber Celestial Angel

© 2024 Amber Celestial Angel

All Rights Reserved.

No part of this material may be reproduced in any way without permission.

celestialangel11118888@gmail.com

linkedin.com/amber-celestial-angel

Donations: paypal.me/ambercelestialangel

ISBN: 9798340934420

Dedicated To:

The Most High God, Yeshua The Messiah and The Sacred Heart, Holy Spirit, Our Heavenly Guides and Angels, and All of His Children and Co Heirs. My One True Love through All Space and Time, From the Beginning, and My Children The Most High has Entrusted me with here on Earth, Lincoln, Thaddeus, and Jaiden.

"The Lord hath appeared of old unto me, saying, Yea, I have loved thee with an everlasting love: therefore with lovingkindness have I drawn thee"

~Jeremiah 31:3

Table of Contents

Intro	5
Prayer of Faith	7
It Is Written	8
Old/Before	10
New/After	75
Wisdom	131
Love	154
Letter of Faith	186
Tale As Old As Time	187

Intro

Growth takes time. We start as a seed, we sprout, we grow, we blossom, and we bloom. Our vibrancy exuding, reaching for The Light, after all, it's what nourishes and feeds us, just as water revitalizes us and helps us grow. This process is not easy.

Like the caterpillar, once walking about grazing on leaves, then progressing into a cocoon, a chrysalis, turning into a liquid, completely disintegrating itself, struggling to emerge and then metamorphosize into a magnificent, flying creature, now sucking on the sweetness of nectar, we too must face the dark, break ourselves apart, and reach for The Light to transform us and sustain us! From that darkness, that pain, that truth, we rise and reach for The Light, coming closer and closer until our wings grasp that Light, and we are completely transformed. Like the phoenix rising from the ashes. We Rise and we Shine, then carry that Light that we worked so hard to gain, gather and sustain. And what is The Source of that Light? It is God. It is Love.

It is what we have always been, always had, but that was hidden away under the darkness that had been cast upon us. It was the missing piece/peace that felt like a void as we slumbered in the void.

But no more! For you see, once One has awakened and seen The Light, they yearn for it, they crave it, for it is The Source of Life, and is the only place One can truly call Home. The Soul craves its Home, where it was created, by The One Magnificent, Almighty Creator.

In the process of Transformation, we learn that Perfect Love casts out all fear. We learn we have to endure the darkness, face the fear, so we can appreciate and see The Light more clearly. So we could know what it was like without it. Only then, once One has gone through the dark (descend), could One reach for The Light (ascend). And through that darkness, we are and never were alone. Christs guiding Light is always with us as we navigate and walk through the valley of the shadow of death, and He brings us out the other side, Into The Light of our Heavenly Abode.

Once we become the renewed (wo)man, we find solace in the understanding of it all. We count it all joy. We are ready to return to the Place we call Home, looking on the unseen, resting in the comfort, harmony, bliss, Agape Love, in The Kingdom of Heaven His Light has led us to, yet remembering and appreciating what was of this Earth for all its Beauty and Splendor. In the Unity of All, in All of the Unity. The dark, The Light, The Alpha, The Omega. All Joined Into One, In the Stillness, the Harmony of Nothing and Everything, Right Here, Right Now. In The Center of Being, In The Heart, where It Is Written.

The Soul(Son) Shines Brightly after the Transformation, and then becomes the Beacon for other Souls to remember their place Among The Heavens, where all are Destined to Return. For He does not want any of His Children to perish. This is Redemption, this is Salvation, this is Freedom, this is Deliverance. This is Coming

Home, Heart In Heart with God, In Everlasting Love,
Hand In Hand, Into The Kingdom of Heaven where we
share Eternal Life.

From Ashes to Beauty,
Are You Ready to Be Transformed?

Prayer of Faith:
Oh Good Lord,
Help me to surrender.
Help me to rest in your embrace,
To trust you COMPLETELY.
Help me to "be still and know"
Help this tiny seed know,
Without a doubt,
That it can MOVE MOUNTAINS!
Help me to look upon your creation and be reminded that you provide every need,
And even more abundantly to those who are called,
According to your purpose,
That I have what I need for every good work.
I pray this in Your Mighty and Precious Name of The Most High God, Christ Yeshua,
In Love,
Selah.

It Is Written,
It Is Sealed.
The Book of Life has its Eternal Etching,
Not in stone,
But In The Heart.
This Sealing has been Preserved since Days of Old,
Since Many Times Past,
Since The Beginning.
There must be an End,
For a Beginning to Start.
So,
Where do we Begin?
We Begin where we Started.
In The Beginning,
Let There Be Light.
The Perfect Image of Him,
Our Creator.
For God Is Love.
Eternal,
Everlasting Love.
It is The Only Thing that Is Real.
For we Look on what is Unseen,
Those who have Eyes to See,
Let them See.
See where It Is Written,
See where It Is Sealed.

Those who have Ears to Hear,
Let them Hear.
For I have Prepared a Place For You,
And there are Many Dwelling Places Within this Kingdom.
And Where I Go,
You Know,
And The Way,
You Know.
Here I AM,
I AM Here.

This Is My Story, This Is My Song....

"Ashes to Beauty"

Mend my Broken Heart,

O Sovereign One,

as Only You can do.

Purify it and Create a Clean Heart within me.

Open the Eyes of my Heart to See All of You.

Turn my Mourning Into Joy,

O Sovereign One,

As Only You can do.

Take this Bottle of Tears,

As I Pour it Upon Your Feet.

Please Comfort me,

And Pour Your Oil Upon my Head.

Take and Lift this Heaviness,

O Sovereign One,

As Only You can do.

Lift my Hands, as I Lift my Eyes to You,

Sight Set High.

Give me Breath,

Give me Life to Raise my Voice in Song to You.

Take these Ashes,

O Sovereign One,

As Only You can do,

And Turn them Into Beauty.

"Invite Me In"

Invite Me In.

Let Me Show you how I Work.

Let Me Show you the Miracles I have for you.

Let Me Show you the Treasures I have in Store for you.

Let Me Show you, Dear Child.

Let Me In.

I'm standing at your gate, at your door, at your window.

I've been Knocking.

I've been Shining My Light, Hoping you would See Me.

Some days you acknowledge Me,

Other days it's as if I was never there.

I'm asking you, to Invite Me In.

Invite Me In Everyday.

Invite Me to Go with you, Everywhere you Go.

When you Invite Me In, I AM able to Show you Wonders.

I AM able to Fill Your Heart with Joy and Laughter,

And In Turn, Spread it to Others who Share Our
Company.

When you Invite Me In,

In All Areas of your Life,

I give All Your Life Reason, Purpose and Meaning,

And the Endurance to Pursue it.

For with Me, All Things are Possible.

Invite Me In,

So I can Give you The Promises.

Let Me Live With You.

Let Me Live Through You.

All you have to do,

Is Let Me In.

"Draw Near"

Draw Near to Me,

I will Keep you Safe.

Come Rest in My Warm,

Soft,

Sweet Embrace.

I will Shelter you.

I won't let any harm or destruction come upon you,

So long as you Stay Close to Me.

For Perfect Love casts out all fear.

There is Only Life here,

With Me.

I AM your Right Hand and your Rear Guard.

I AM the All Encompassing Safehouse and Sanctuary.

You can Rest Assure knowing I AM The Place of Rest.

You can have Peace of Mind knowing I AM that of a Sound Mind.

Just keep Drawing Near to Me,

Closer and Closer,

Ever Present in this Present Moment with Me,

As I Shine Within You.

"Fall Into Me"

Fall Into Me.

Fall Into My Arms.

Let Me Hold you.

Let My Warm, Soft Embrace Surround you,

And become One with You.

Sink Into My Love,

Fully Embrace Me.

It's My Love that I want to Give You,

That I want to Hold You In,

So Let Me.

Accept Me and Let Me Love You.

You can Trust Me.

You can Confide In Me.

Come to Me, My Darling, My Child, My Love.

Come to Me and Let Me Love You the way You are Meant to be Loved.

You are Worthy of My Love,

For I have Loved You with an Everlasting Love that has No Bounds.

I AM in You, and All Around You,

Always.

I AM Your Fortress,

Your Shelter,

Your Comfort,

And You can Give All of Yourself to Me,

Completely.

For I AM Yours,

The Same Way that You are Mine.

Receive Me and My Gift, My Love,

It's Specially Made, Just for You.

"Let the Wall Fall"

I thought I had built my wall so strong, so mighty.

I thought those walls would protect me and guard me.

It took a long time to build them.

It didn't take much to sustain them though.

People came and left,

They had their walls too.

Everyone so guarded, so protected from themselves and God.

So, they proved my walls could stay.

Until I met You….

My whole World changed.

My walls came tumbling, crumbling,

Piece by piece,

Stone by stone they fell.

I wanted to catch them and try to save them,

Wanting to build it back up,

But I couldn't.

As the walls fell, I felt more and more Free.

I crave Freedom more than chains.

So as the wall was crumbling,

I saw myself dying.

Pieces of me dying.

They needed to die,

Because they were only keeping me caged.

A Free Bird cannot be caged.

But I had to see the wall in the first place,

Once I did, I knew it had to Come Down.

And it's Your Love that did it,

That tore down those walls and Set Me Free.

The One thing that withstands Through All Space and Time…

Love.

Your Unconditional Love Tore My World Apart,

And I wouldn't have it any other way.

For You are My Strength and My Refuge.

You are My Foundation.

The New Foundation that Makes Way for The New Jerusalem.

The Kingdom.

I have Found My Home,

Thanks to You,

Oh Almighty One,

Thanks to You.

"Fall Completely"

All the pieces had to Fall Away,

All the stones had to Crumble,

The whole wall had to Fall Down,

Just so You could Build Me Up,

On a Steady, Firm Foundation.

I had to Face the Depths of Myself,

Had to Face the Dark.

All the While Your Light, Your Love,

Was Leading me Through it All.

You were Always There,

Holding me,

Guiding me,

Protecting me.

I was Never Alone. I AM Never Alone.

All I had to go through,

Only Helped my Endurance,

And Steadfast Faith in You.

It All Drew me Closer and Closer,

More In Love With You.

Your Unconditional Love is My Strength.

You Leave No Stone Unturned,

And Through it All,

I Rest in Your Embrace,

For I Know Your Yoke is Easy,

Your Burden is Light.

You Carry me in the Storm,

Upon a Peaceful Sea.

I See the Beauty in All the Trials and Tribulations.

I See the Beauty of Now, where it has gotten me.

And I See the Beauty that is Yet to Come,

Because I Know with You, I can Face ANYTHING!

"Many Trials"

I have been through many trials,

Pressed down and shaken,

Broken and shattered,

Torn and ripped apart,

Only to Find You.

Through All the many struggles and strife,

It only Brought Me Closer and Closer to You.

Strengthening My Faith in You,

Strengthening My Trust in You,

Strengthening My Hope in Your Promises.

Building My Endurance and Perseverance in Your Name,

In the Truth of Who I AM,

Who You Are,

Who We Are.

Thank You for tearing me down,

So You could Build Me Back Up,

Stronger,

Wiser,

Grander,

More Prosperous and Fruitful,

More Firm and Stable In You,

In Your Everlasting Life and Love.

"Broken"

My Heart has been broken.

It has Yearned for You a thousand times,

And a thousand more over.

But I have come to find Rest in the Solace of My Heart,

The Place where The Light has Entered,

After the cracks had to Be Bestowed.

For how could I have known a Love So Deeply,

So Purely,

Without having Missed It?

It had to hurt,

It had to break for me to Find You.

You were Always There,

But I didn't know it,

Until I Knew You.

And for me to Know You,

I had to die.

I had to be in pain.

I had to suffer.

And I had to die over and over again,

To Finally, Truly Live.

My Heart has Become more and more like The Olive Tree,

Having to Tend it Year after Year.

80 to Mature.

What Loyalty this Takes.

And it Only Grows Stronger and Wiser with Each Passing Year,

Each Passage of Time.

The Hands that Tend this Garden,

This Heart,

Have to Be Quit Mighty to withstand,

And they are.

They are The Hands of The Almighty,

Who Directs Our Every Step,

Every Move.

He is The Tender,

He is The True Vine,

We are The Gardener.

With His Direction and Guidance,

We are Never Led Astray.

My Garden,

My Heart,

Remains Pure and True in His Hands.

I Know He Holds Me Preciously.

"Come"

Come with Me, My Darling.

Take My Hand as I Lead You to Fine Green Pastures,

Where Fields of Lillies and Roses Spring Abound,

And Dance in an Array of Color.

Where The Willow, Oak and Cedar Stand Wise, Strong and Tall,

Among the Lush Green Land.

With Rolling Hills, and Pure, Fresh Air sent straight from Heaven Above.

Take this Breath of Life I Give You,

So Willingly,

So Freely,

Take It, My Love.

Come with Me, My Darling,

To the Crisp Sparkling Waters,

Where My Spirit is Poured Upon You,

And You are Refreshed and Revitalized.

Drink with Me from The Chalice I offer You, My Love.

See, Your Reflection Is Mine,

I AM In You.

You Carry this Light that I Lead You with.

I AM Your Refuge.

Stay Strong and Faithful In Me, and My Light Will Shine Brighter and Brighter Through You.

Come with Me, My Darling.

Walk with Me, and My Lamp will Light Your Way.

Take Shelter Under My Wings and Trust that I will Hold You Close,

And Never Lead You Astray.

You have My Word,

A Lamp Unto Your Feet, a Light Unto Your Path.

Come with Me, My Darling.

Take the Leap of Faith and Fully Surrender, Give Me Your Life.

I will Resurrect it and Transform You into a Renewed Being,

Pure, Clean, and Without Blemish,

So You can Experience the Miracles set Beside you and Before you.

Come with Me, My Darling, I'm Right Here.

"My Sacrifice"

The Greatest Sacrifice I can Offer You,

Is My Heart.

There is No Greater Treasure.

For where Thy Treasure is,

There Thine Heart also is.

It is The Life Force of this body,

It is what keeps One Alive.

It takes Great Courage for one to Give their Heart,

It is a Delicacy.

For many it has been battered and bruised,

Bent and broken.

So for One to Give it Openly,

Wholly,

Fully,

Is The Highest Form of Sacrifice,

In deed.

From it Flows my tears,

My pain,

My Joy,

My Praise.

From it Your Words of Wisdom Guide another Home,

To You,

Where they can also choose to Relinquish their Heart to You.

Truly,

It is Only when we Give Our Heart to You,

That we are Truly Alive.

If My Heart is not Your Heart,

Then I have No Life.

At least not one that is worth living.

Therefore,

I put My Life In Your Hands.

I Give You My Heart.

My Greatest Sacrifice,

I AM All Yours.

"Surrender"

I had to go to The Depths of My Soul to Find You.

I had to Dig so Deep to find those Old Wounds.

And when I Went There,

You Gave me the Courage and Bravery to Face them.

That took a lot for me to Face.

But I knew with Your Protection,

Your Shield,

Your Helmet,

With my Trust,

My Faith,

My Courage,

I Knew We could do it.

So I have done it.

I have Surrendered to You.

Everyday,

In Everything I do.

I let You Take the Wheel,

Even though it may be a Blind Drive ahead,

I Trust in Your Knowing Better than I.

You Show Me You are Here Every Step of The Way.

I Follow Your Footprints In The Sand.

You Lead,

You Stand Beside Me,

You Live Within Me.

Everyday I Give My Life To You,

So I can Truly Live.

Everyday I die,

So I can Surrender Into Your Soft,

Sweet Embrace in the Place of Flow,

Where You Carry Me Along The River,

Cleansing Me In Your Waters and Making Me New Again.

My Salvation,

My Redemption,

My Deliverance.

I Love You with Every Ounce of My Being.

With My Body,

Mind,

Spirit,

And Soul.

I Give it to You.

I Give it to You.

Selah.

"I See Clearly"

How did I not See Your Value?

How did it slip by, how Important it is that You are in My Life.

I was lost without you,

You Found Me,

And I still didn't See how much I Needed You,

Even when You were Right There.

I guess I took You for granted.

I thought You would Always Be There,

And while it's True, You Are,

I had to See past myself,

To Really See You.

I had to Open My Eyes and Look Clearly Into You.

It's as if I was on auto pilot,

Just going about my days blinded,

Seeing only what I wanted to see,

And not what You were trying to Show Me.

You were Always Trying to Take My Hand and Lead Me the Right Way,

But many times I fell astray and wondered away.

Sometimes even running away.

But even so,

You Continued Reaching for My Hand,

Continued Loving Me and Trying.

I See Clearly Now,

Just how much You have Been Here For Me,

How much You have Never Left Me.

Your Grace,

Mercy,

Forgiveness,

Has Given Me a New Sight,

Where I can Finally See how I can Trust Your Guidance for the Rest of My Days.

Thank You God,

You have Restored My Sight.

I See The Light.

"Peel the Layers"

You had to peel every layer,

Shedding,

Releasing.

More shedding,

More releasing.

Every piece of me had to be stripped away for me to Walk with You,

In Your Way,

Your Truth,

Your Light.

Layer by layer you peeled me,

And with each peel, it hurt,

It tore me,

But with every layer that had been peeled,

A New One grew Healthier,

Stronger,

More Renewed,

More Beautiful.

It was Only You who could've done it,

Only You.

They say that with every heartbreak, it Heals,

And while they are right,

What they forget to mention is that it also brings us Closer to You,

More in Your Grace, Mercy and Love,

Than the time before.

With every tear,

Every trouble,

Every pain,

We Fall more and more Into Your Arms,

We Rise more and more In Your Love.

My Shepherd, My Guide,

You Carry Me along Green Pastures,

You Feed Me with Your Words of Strength, Hope, Faith, Perseverance, Truth, Wisdom, and Above All, Love.

And as I Rise,

More and More In Love with You,

You Prove, Time and Time again,

Love Never Fails.

Love Conquers All.

So as I Rest in Your Wings of Refuge,

I Trust You,

I Know You.

I Feel You.

You are with Me,

Always and Forevermore.

"Give All"

I Humbly and Joyfully Give to You.

I Give it All to You.

I trade the sorrow, guilt, shame, pain and trouble

For the only thing You can Bring.

That is,

Joy, Mercy, Grace, Peace, Pure Love.

You take my burdens and Carry them,

So I can be Free of the weight,

And in turn, I Become Lighter and Lighter.

Light as a Feather,

A Feather Under Your Wings,

Where You keep me Nestled and Safe.

Your Forgiveness Grants me Freedom and Hope.

You Set me Free from past mistakes,

You Continue having Patience, Grace and Mercy with me.

And with that, I AM Free.

You Prove Your Light and Your Mighty Love by taking those burdens,

And Showing me the Bright Future with You,

Right Beside me,

Leading me every step of The Way.

Every step becoming Lighter and Brighter as You Carry Me all The Way Home.

"Journey Home"

I Hold Onto The Promise of what The Almighty has for me,

Yet I AM content with what He has already Bestowed Upon me.

With much Patience and Endurance,

I AM Guided by His Hand,

Enjoying The Walk we have Together.

Slow and Steady,

Nice and Easy,

We Walk,

We Dance,

We Skip Along The Way Home.

And I AM Home Right Now,

Where He is With Me,

In The Heart.

Sometimes The Journey can be tiring, and I need to Rest,

So I Rest in The Refuge of His Mighty Wings.

Sometimes it rains,

And I AM Under His Umbrella,

Other times We Enjoy Dancing in the rain.

No matter what,

I Keep My Eyes on The Prize,

The Rainbow.

That Beautiful Sight to Behold.

Just as He Holds Me All Along The Journey,

Sometimes even Carrying Me,

I Thank Him for Always Being There. Here.

I Thank Him for having Patience with me,

And for my Patience Growing, too.

I Thank Him for Lighting My Way so I never get lost as we make Our Way Home,

And what a Miraculous Place it is!

"Leading, Guiding"

As I Walk with You Beside me,

Hand in Hand,

Each New Day,

I Know You are also Ahead of me,

Leading The Way.

Your Footsteps of Grace, Beauty, Splendor and Wonder
Light The Path Before me.

All of Creation is Marveled at Your Majesty,

And so long as You are My Guide,

I get to be a part of the Marvelous Majesty You Bestow
Upon All.

You Lead me to The Well,

Where I will drink and Be Cleansed,

Each New Day,

Each New Season, that You have Planned for me.

I Follow You, O Holy One,

O Marvelous King,

O Joyous Creator,

I Follow You,

And I Know My Path is Straight and Filled with Blessings and Wondrous Sights along The Way.

I Smile with the rising of the sun,

And the going down the same,

Knowing that You are Here with Me,

Knowing that tomorrow, whatever it may bring,

I can get through it because of You,

"You See?"

Can't you See?

It's Right Here,

Right Now,

This very Magnificent Moment.

At this very Moment I AM Working In You,

Through You.

I AM Building You,

I AM Nurturing You.

You are Growing Right Now.

With each Moment, it is Growth.

You may not see it Now, but You Will.

Growth,

Transformation,

Takes Time.

This Time is but a Flicker,

A Flash,

And still yet,

In this Moment,

It's as if Time is Still.

Don't rush this Time,

For it is Imperative for Growth and Understanding.

You wouldn't expect a Seed you Planted today to Grow overnight,

Would You?

No, it takes Time.

Nurturing,

Watering,

Loving.

It's a Process.

And with The Light of Each New Day,

Begins its Transformation.

So, You See,

How much this very Now Moment Means?

It is The Moment that is in this very Space and Place in Time,

That while it is only a Glimmer,

It Matters.

Creation,

Growth,

Transformation,

Miracles,

Are Happening Right Now.

They Will Blossom and Show Themselves in Time.

For Right Now You Once Prayed,

Hoped,

Dreamed,

That You would be Right where You Are Now.

Enjoy this Now Moment,

It Only Happens Once in a Lifetime.

"Eye See You"

Right Here is where Eye See You,

Where I Know You.

I'm walking, keeping my Gaze Ahead,

Right Here,

Where I AM,

Seeing everything around me,

Seeing You all around me.

Your Pristine Beauty,

Your Miracles.

I Hear You in the Waves of the Water,

Or in the Tune of a Cardinal,

Singing Her Tune for Her Mate to Follow.

I Feel You in My Heart,

Beating as One with Yours.

You are My Sunshine,

You are My Rain,

You are My Rainbow.

You are My Everything,

Christ, My King, My Good God Almighty.

You Bring Peace and Harmony,

You Bring Balance and Bliss.

I AM with You Forevermore,

As are You with Me, Forevermore.

You are My Home,

And I will always Return to You,

At Your Feet.

"Looking Up"

I'm Still Looking Up.

Though I Walk through the Valley of (the shadow of) death,

I Know Thou Art With Me.

Thy Rod and Staff Comfort Me as I Walk By Faith,

Not By Sight.

As You Lead Me, One Step at a Time,

I Keep My Gaze Fixed Upon You.

I may not See the Full Path Ahead,

But I Trust You will Light The Way as Each Step is Taken.

As I Walk Through The Valley,

I Know Thou Art With Me,

For How could there be a shadow,

If there were no Light?

A Cloud by Day,

A Pillar by Night.

I Know You Will not forsake Me,

O YHWH My God,

For You are My Strength,

You are My Light,

You are My Love,

You,

Are All I Need.

"At Your Feet"

Whenever I feel hopeless or in despair,

I come to You, O Love,

O My God.

I Bow in Reverence to You,

And my tears flow upon Your Feet.

You Gather them,

Cherish them,

And Use them in The River as they Cleanse and Heal My Soul,

And those Souls whom I have shed these tears for.

You Renew My Hope,

Reminding me of Your Promise,

Reminding me how Right Now I AM in Your Mighty Hands and Your Precious Love.

You Hold me so Closely,

So Warmly.

You put my mind at Ease.

You bring Peace to My Being.

You bring me back to the Place I call Home,

In Your Pure,

True Love,

Where We Abide as One.

So while I may feel down momentarily,

Your Mighty Love Lifts Me Up,

Where We Dwell in the Fortress of Pure,

Heavenly Presence of Oneness,

O what a Place to BE!

"Release"

I Release the bands of bondage.

I Release the chains of slavery.

I Release the cords of wickedness.

I Break Off Every Yoke!

I Will Not be hurt.

I Will Not be humiliated.

I Will Not be put to shame.

No Weapon formed against Me shall prosper.

You Bring Justice and Judgment.

You have Given Me Peace.

You have Given Me Freedom.

You have Given Me Grace.

For Your Yoke Is Easy, and Your Burden Is Light.

By Your Will I AM Healed.

By Your Will I AM Humble.

By Your Will I AM Forgiven.

For Light Dawns in the darkness,

Shining Brightly as Noonday,

Continually Guiding My Steps,

Lighting Up The Way.

"Restore"

You have Restored My Song.

You have Restored My Innocence.

You have Restored My Mind.

You have Restored My Voice.

You have Restored My Truth.

You have Restored My Life.

You have Restored My Soul.

You have Restored All of Me.

I AM Holy and Complete.

Thank You.

"Deliver"

Deliverance has Come!

As You say in Your Word,

"Shall I make a Promise, and not Deliver?"

Of course You do!

As sure as Your Word goes forth,

It does not return void,

But does Your Will,

Accomplishing what You Sent it for.

Your Promises Always Stand,

You Always Stand on Your Word!

As Promised,

You have Delivered Me from the bondage,

Set Me Free,

And Lead Me Into The Promised Land.

Fear has No Hold on Me,

Your Grace and Love Own Me Now,

For Perfect Love casteth out All fear!

"Deliver Thy Enemy"

I AM Preserved Under The Shadow of Your Wings.

You Keep Me Safe in The Haven of Your Love.

While thy enemy may be on the prowl,

Seeking to devour,

I AM Hidden in Your Mighty Fortress.

You have Given Me Peace,

Stillness and Silence,

And The Power of Prayer to Tame the beast.

As he slithers slyly,

Watching,

Waiting to strike,

You have Given Me the High View,

The Eyes to Spot him,

And The Power to Cast him Down Under Thy Feet.

I AM not safe because of the absence of evil,

I AM Safe because of Your Presence,

O God,

And You Fight My Battles For Me.

For You Strike as Lightening and Shine Your Face Upon Thy enemy,

Bringing him to his knees in Repentance and Deliverance.

I Rejoice in his Deliverance to You!

May Your Grace Light his way,

And Your Glory Shine Upon him!

HalleluYah!

"Grace, Grit, Glory"

You Give Grace,

Which Builds Character with Grit and Magnifies Your Glory.

Your Amazing Grace has taught me what True Forgiveness is.

It has taught me how to Have Mercy.

It has Paved The Way to True Repentance,

Where You have taught me how to Have Grit.

This Grit has Helped me Persevere and Stand Bravely and Courageously against the adversary.

It has Helped me Stand Firm in You,

Knowing I can face Anything with Your Strength,

Your Grace,

Your Word,

Your Glory.

Your Glory has Overcome My Being and Clothed Me in Your Esteem.

It has Renewed Me Into The New,

Where,

Because of You,

I Give ALL Glory to You

For without these things,

I would be in shame,

I would be broken,

I would be lost.

But because You have Shown me,

I AM Saved,

By Grace,

Through Grit,

And With Glory.

"Glory to Greater Glory"

From Glory to Greater Glory You Renew Me.

Each trial that has been Endured and Pressed On Steadfastly,

Has Only Brought Me More and More Into Your Glorious Kingdom.

Where Your Light Esteems and Exalts the Accomplishments,

Which could Only Be Achieved because of Your Astounding Glory.

Glory which You have Granted with each Passing of the Tests,

With Each Test Proving Firm and Greater Faith.

Every trial Faced and Endured,

Only Brings Greater Glory,

Higher Esteem,

And More Praise to Your Name and Your Kingdom.

My Steps are Your Steps,

My Gain is Your Gain.

For it is Only You whom All the Glory Belongs to.

I AM The Beacon on The Hill,

Oh My God,

But You,

You are The Burning Bush.

"Resilient"

I AM Resilient.

I have been held captive.

I have been broken hearted.

I have been tossed about the stormy sea.

I have been pressed down and shaken.

I have been a lost sheep.

But You...

You Set Me Free.

You Bound My broken heart.

You Calmed the sea.

You Refined Me.

You Found Me.

Through it All,

You have been With Me.

You have Strengthened Me.

You have made sure I Endured.

You have Taken Down the strongholds,

And Cast Them Into The Light,

Where I must Face them...

Mighty is He in the Pulling Down of strongholds...

"Into Your Light"

Out of darkness, Into Your Marvelous Light I See Clearly.

You have Shone Me The Light.

I must Face You, I must Look at The Light.

The Veil has Been Lifted and Your Truth has Been Revealed.

It hurts to Look, but I must Face It.

I can Only Face it With You,

For I cannot Look Into Your Holiness without The Holiness of Christ and The Sacred Heart.

This is the Only Way to Face it...

With Love.

With Mercy.

With Grace.

For You did not come to condemn, but to Save.

I AM Free from condemnation,

And I AM Set Free from sin ONLY because of Mercy and Grace which has been Given,

Because You have Loved Me with an Everlasting Love.

So Much So, That You Died,

For Me.

I Receive You,

Holy and Fully.

All The Truth, The Light, The Love.

I SEE The Burning Bush,

And I Look Upon Your Excellence.

I Marvel at Your Glory and Esteem.

I Face Your "White Hot" Light,

A Fire So Pure,

So Fierce.

Although some days I don't feel worthy,

I AM reminded that I AM Worthy because I AM that Reflection.

I must Face You if I want to Face Me.

If I want to Become Purified,

Refined,

Holy,

Then I must Flow with The Current.

I must Face the Fire.

I must Withstand The Heat,

The Pressure,

The Brightness of Your Magnificence.

I am not afraid.

You have Lifted The Veil,

I have Seen Your Face,

And I AM Ready to Cross The Threshold,

I AM Ready To Walk On Water,

For I Know You Are With Me.

"Eye of the Storm"

In the Eye of the Storm,

I AM Still.

While there is chaos and debris all around,

You bring a Peace that Surpasses All Understanding.

I AM Abiding in a Quiet Place,

A Space Outside of Time,

Where We are One.

I and The Father are One,

You and I are One.

In this Calm in the midst of a raging storm,

I AM Held so Firmly,

So Comfortably.

Oh My Soul is as Free as The Eagle,

Soaring High Above the Lands,

Floating,

Resting.

At the Same Time, You Carry me Through,

Lighting Our Way.

I AM Safe with You.

For surely after the storms have settled,

The Sun shall Shine Again,

And The Rainbow shall Color The Sky,

And I shall Dance and Rejoice Amongst The Clouds.

After all,

The Son was Never Gone,

And He was Holding the Rainbow the Whole Time!

"Into the New, Indeed"

You are My Anchor.

My Faith is Firm and Stable in You.

As I rock and roll with the tide,

As I fight against the waves,

I Still Know that You are Right Here Carrying me Through The Storm.

Just as The Ship Sails Through The Raging Storm,

The Winds rocking The Vessel to and fro,

The Tides shifting high and low,

So too is the old man being rocked to and fro,

Being brought high and low.

The flesh and The Spirit at odds.

The old trying to hang on.

The chains trying to wrap back around after being broken.

But the old must die.

It Is Dead!

No matter how much is trying to hang on,

I Let it Go!

No matter how much the chains keep trying to wrap back around,

I have Totally Broken them!

But Only With You.

For You are The Only One who can Set Me Free.

You are The Only One who Has Set Me Free.

For whosoever The Son Sets Free,

Is Free Indeed.

So Surely, I AM Free,

And The New Deed is Fruitful and Everlasting.

It is Living,

Holy and Pure.

The New Deed is Anchored Upon a Ship that Sails Beyond the sea and Into Heavenly Places,

Where no matter what the weather,

The Rainbow is it's Guiding Light

2 Corintheans 5:17

"Therefore, if anyone is in Christ, he is a new creation, old things have passed away; behold all things have become new."

"Slay the Dragon"

Was it Not You Who Pierced the dragon?

Who Cut pride Apart?

It Was....

It Was I Who went to The Depths of The Sea to Face the dragon of leviathan.

The biggest monster of The Sea,

Who had taken many souls asunder.

But with The Love of God,

With The Son of God,

With The Courage to face him,

To face thy self of flesh,

He has been slain!

I could Not Do this Alone,

As a man.

I had to shed the flesh and Call Upon Christ and His Holiness,

I had to have Our Angels as My Rear Guard,

I had to Let Go of the man,

And I had to Accept The Christ.

Only then could the beast be slain.

For what God Puts Together,

Let no man tear apart!

When We Are United In Christ,

In The Sacred Heart,

With God,

All Things Are Possible.

What seemed a task impossible,

Was Accomplished the Only Way it Could Be,

With Him.

I AM stripped of the flesh,

And Forevermore Filled With The Love of God,

In The Immaculate Heart,

One With All,

Set Free!

"Victory"

I can do All Things Through You, Christ, Messiah, who Strengthens Me,

For You are Within Me.

My Power, is not my own,

But it is You Within Me.

My Strength, is not my own,

But it is You Within Me.

I AM that I AM.

You have Helped me face my fears,

Face myself,

Face the adversary,

Giving me the Full Armour,

Teaching Me,

Equipping Me,

Preparing Me,

And I Know with You,

Victory is Always at Hand.

It is Always the Destination,

For I Give All to You,

Knowing,

Trusting,

Believing,

That the Battle is Won before it has Begun.

Only because of You,

Only with You,

Is Victory Promised.

No matter how long it takes,

I will Endure.

No matter how hard the task,

I will Accomplish.

No matter how tired I may get,

I will Stay Awake.

For You are My Rock,

My Steady, Firm Foundation.

You are My Shield,

My Mighty Protection.

You are My Refuge,

Upholding Me in Your Arms.

Together,

We are Untouchable.

United We Stand.

"I AM Free"

Through Your Mighty Love You have Freed Me.

I was held captive,

In bondage,

Held in chains,

But You,

Oh Almighty One,

You Set Me Free.

You broke the chains,

You ripped the bondage,

And You Set Me Free.

You Redeemed Me,

And You Brought Salvation to Me.

Only You Can.

Only You Have,

And I Thank You for Never Giving Up on Me,

For having Patience with Me,

For having Mercy on Me.

You have Always Walked with Me.

You have never left Me.

You have Always been Here,

Beside Me,

Within Me,

And Above Me.

You have Heard Me,

Heard My Prayers,

My Thanks,

My Heart.

It Beats to the Rhythm of Your Love,

Your Truth.

It Beats because of You.

For without You I would have no life,

Without You I would be lost,

Without You I would be incomplete.

You Give Me Life,

You Found Me,

I Found You,

You Complete Me.

Because of You,

I AM FREE.

Because of You,

I AM ALIVE.

Because of You,

I AM WELL.

The walls were torn down,

To Rebuild the New.

You are My Foundation,

You are My Rock.

I Rest and Live In You.

"Rooted and Grounded In Love"

We got Deep and dug up the Roots.

We had to Go Deep,

Sift through the Soil,

and get every little root,

Even the ones we couldn't See,

The ones that were hiding.

As we dug we were faced with times of darkness,

But The Light was ALWAYS SHINING THROUGH!

Your Word was a Lamp unto Thy Feet,

A Light unto Thy Path.

Your Love Held a Torch that burned Through the darkness.

The Soil was Purified and Cleansed,

Burned for Purification,

Watered for Cleansing.

Once that Process took Place,

It was Time to Plant New Seeds.

Fresh Soil, Fresh Seeds.

Rooted and Grounded In Love.

A New Beginning for an Abundant and Flourishing Harvest.

"New Wineskin"

I had to clear out the old storehouses and shed the old wineskin so the New could Enter.

New Wineskin, Full Storehouse.

A Storehouse, a Sanctuary, a Temple,

Dedicated to You, O Yah.

For You are The Landlord of The Storehouse,

The Peace of The Sanctuary,

The God of This Temple.

It took a lot of Sacrifice,

Dedication,

Perseverance,

Endurance,

And Failure,

Over and Over again,

To Finally get to a Clean Space for You to Start Over with.

But Once it Finally happened, a Clean Slate,

A Clean House,

So much weight was lifted,

And Your Light was able to Shine Through,

So much Lighter and Brighter.

You Created a Clean Heart Within Me,

And a Steadfast Spirit that Only With You could've been done.

I was able to Receive You Deeper,

And Receive the New Wineskin.

I was able to Receive My Crown,

Holy and Fully,

Which you So Tenderly,

Mercifully,

Gracefully,

Patiently,

Placed Upon My Head.

Thank you, Oh Mighty One,

For Being With Me,

Walking With Me,

Hand in Hand,

And Leading Me Down The Straight Path,

Walking Me Into The Promised Land,

My Love,

My King,

Thank You.

"Breath of Life"

You are My Breath.

You are My Heartbeat.

You are My Life.

I AM Alive because of You.

I AM nothing without You, non existent.

I look back to the past,

And I see I had nothing,

Because I didn't have You.

I Stand Here Now

And I See I have Everything,

Because I have You.

I look ahead and I See nothing matters if you're not there,

Here,

Within Me.

You are The Only Way,

Today and Tomorrow.

You're all I See,

Wherever I go,

And wherever that is,

I know I'm going The Right Way,

As long as I have You.

You brought me to Redemption,

You bring me to Salvation.

You Scorned me in The Fire,

And You Cleansed me in The Water.

You have Shown me Mercy,

Shown me Grace,

Shown me Compassion,

Shown me Patience,

Shown me Thankfulness,

And Above All,

Shown me Love.

For without The Love,

Nothing else would be possible.

I could know You without it,

But I couldn't Experience The Depth of You without it.

I couldn't Carry The Light,

The Heart,

The Holy Spirit Fire, without You.

You are It, Christ,

My King,

The Only Way.

I Finally Found You,

You Found Me,

Never Giving Up.

And Here I AM,

With You Now, and Forevermore.

"Lost Without You"

I would be lost without You.

I was lost without You.

You were the missing piece that I had longed for,

Not even realizing I needed You.

You opened My Heart and Showed me Real, True Love.

I never knew it was possible,

But once You Turned the Key and Opened that Door,

There was no closing it.

The Profound Love that You Showed me,

That I've felt Deep Within Me,

Has Awakened and now can slumber no more.

For once One has been Bathed in this Pure, True Love,

One cannot turn away from It.

For if One tries to turn away,

It only hurts and makes one long for It again.

I wasn't searching, so I thought,

But You Found Me anyway.

You knew what I needed, long before I did.

You knew My Heart from the Day I was Born.

You knew Your Plan for me long before I did.

How did You Find Me?

In a World of so many lost souls,

You Found Me!

How Glorious to be the Apple of Your Eye,

And for out of the 99, you never forgot about the One.

Thank You.

Thank You for Finding Me, and Never Giving up on Me.

Now I AM Found and Returning Home, To You.

"Will You Come Home?"

To Those who will Accept,

Those who Have The Heart to Love Once Again,

Those Ready to Be Washed Clean,

You are Invited to Return Home.

To Come to The Table,

Where All are Always Welcome and Wanted.

Where All are Accepted and Loved.

For His Love,

His Grace,

His Forgiveness has No Bounds.

Will You Come to The Table?

There is Always a Place Set,

Just For You.

Will You Return Home?

The Light is Always On,

Just For You.

For You,

Dear One,

You Are Worthy.

"Will You Serve"

I Walk Worthily of The Calling for which You have Set Forth for My Destiny.

Though it has not been easy,

For I have felt that I don't deserve a place at Your Table.

But You Quickly Remind me that I AM Always Welcome,

Always Worthy of Your Sweet Love.

For I AM the Apple of Your Eye,

In The Image and Likeness of You,

So how could I not Be Worthy?

You Remind me I AM not of this world,

No,

But I AM Chosen,

I AM Peculiar,

I AM Yours,

A Child of The Most High,

One with All that You Are.

You Set Me Apart,

You Called Me to Serve You,

To Serve The Kingdom of Heaven,

And I Humbly and Whole Heartedly Accepted.

Now I AM Free and at Your Service.

The Service of Truth and Love,

Spreading Your Word,

Your Wisdom,

Your Unconditional Love.

To Those who Hear The Call,

Take Your Place at The Table.

"Sight Set"

My Sight is Set On You.

You Bring Me Joy,

Freedom,

Adventure,

Hope,

Truth,

Love.

My Eyes are Fixed Upon You and All The Loveliness You Bring.

You have Shown Me so much Pleasure,

Warmth,

Light,

Grace,

Wisdom.

You have Shown Me darkness,

Shame,

Guilt,

Broken Heartedness,

But only because it had to be Endured for me to Truly SEE You.

So Now,

With My Gaze Fixed Upon You,

Wholly and Completely,

I AM at Your Service,

In Your Name,

The Name of Love.

I have Endured Much,

Only to Bring Me Closer to You.

To Trust You,

To Have Faith In You,

To Believe In You,

To Know You,

To Be Open To Receive You.

You Are My Guiding Light,

My Candle in the darkness,

My Sun that Shines Through with The Dawning of Each New Day.

I Look To You.

And just like The Sun,

You Keep Me Warm and Held.

I Know that whatever is to come,

I can Withstand it,

Because I have You with Me.

You Keep Me Going.

Your Love Keeps Me Going.

And I Know because of Your Love,

That You Bring Blessings and Favour My Way,

For I Serve You.

I Know You want Your Children Happy,

Healthy,

Free With You,

In Your Love.

I See The Blessings and Gifts You have already Given,

Whether they came easy or hard,

I See them.

And I Thank You.

And I Continue to Have My Sight Set On You,

Knowing You are Here,

And You Give Me the Desires of Mine Heart,

In Your Kingdom,

And Here on Earth.

On Earth as It Is In Heaven.

That is The Promise,

And I know it is True,

For You are The Key to It All,

And I Hold The Key.

"Believe"

I Share My Voice with You.

I Share My Heart with You.

You Know All My Secrets,

All My Concerns,

All My Dreams.

You Know it All.

I Know My Voice is Heard By You.

I Know You Hear My Prayers.

For I Know the Earnest Prayers of a Righteous One,

And Prayers from The Heart,

Accomplish Much.

You Know what I Need Before I Ask,

But Still I Ask,

For I Hear You Speak, Saying;

"Ask, Believe, and So Shall You Receive".

I Believe.

I Believe You Hear Me,

In the Good Times,

And in the Hard Times.

And I Believe You Always Answer,

In Your Timing,

Divine Timing.

And Your Divine Appointment is Never too Late,

But Right On Time.

Just as I Call Out to You,

You Call Out to Me, Saying;

"Shh, Be Still and Know. Listen".

In The Stillness,

I Hear You.

I Hear You and See You in Your Beautiful Creation All Around.

I Hear You in a Song You Play For Me,

Or In a Stranger Who Speaks those Perfect Words whom You Gave The Message to Relay.

I Hear You in Your Word I Read Everyday.

Thank You for Being My Light,

Shining The Way.

Thank You for Hearing All I Have to Say.

Thank You for All You Do,

My God,

I Believe In You.

"Devoted"

I AM Devoted to You, O Love.

You are the Center of My Being,

My Life Revolves Around You.

My Life Belongs to You,

For You have Revived My Soul.

There's no place I'd rather be,

Than right here with You, Day and Night.

Your Breath of Life is what keeps me going.

Your Words of Wisdom, Your Word of Truth, is My Guidance.

Day In and Day Out I Live to Serve You, Almighty One.

You are My Redeemer.

My Salvation lies with You,

In Your Precious and Mighty Hands.

I Give All to You,

Knowing You Keep Me Safe and Sheltered in Your Mighty Hands,

And Under Your Mighty Wings.

O Love,

I AM Yours.

You Have All of Me,

And I Have All of You.

"Everlasting Love"

I AM Precious in Your Eyes.

You have Loved me with and Everlasting Love.

Despite all the sins,

Despite missing the mark,

Time and time again,

You still Kept Your Eyes on me.

You still Remained Close to me,

Never leaving me behind.

You took those sins and Washed Them Clean with Your Mercy and Grace.

Your Faith in Me Never Failed.

Your Love Never Failed.

Because of Your Mercy and Grace,

Now I AM Holy,

I AM Pure.

I Hit the Target Every Time,

With My Sight Set on You.

I Only Have Eyes for You.

You are The Apple of My Eye,

Just as I AM Yours.

You have Drawn Me with Your Loving Kindness,

Into Your Everlasting Love and Eternal Life.

With a Sound Mind,

Clean Heart,

And Steadfast Spirit,

I Dance and Sing,

And Rejoice in All Your Glory and Esteem.

I Hold My Hands High,

Open My Heart,

And Lift My Eyes,

Fixed Upon You,

Never Losing Sight,

For Now, I See.

"Faithfully Yours"

You are My Refuge.

I Come to You.

You Keep me Warm.

You Keep me Safe.

You Shelter me with Your Wings.

My Protector.

My Shield.

My Strength.

You Lift me Up when I am down.

You Remind me to Keep Faith,

To Trust and to Know that You are Always Here with me.

You Surround me in Your Mighty Love,

Reminding me how Deep and Strong it is.

How Pure it is.

You Fill my Cup,

And it Runneth Over,

Pouring,

Flowing, Exceedingly,

So that I may Share Your Love Through My Vessel.

I AM Your Vessel, I AM Your Cup.

The more You Heal me,

Purify me,

Cleanse me,

The more Free Flowing and Filled I AM.

Ever Flowing,

Harmoniously,

Eternally.

You have Forged me in The Fire,

You have Washed me Clean.

Pure and Fierce,

The Beauty in The Balance.

The Perfection in The Oneness You bring to My Being.

This Essence Moves me and Exudes me.

I AM Yours, Faithfully, In Love.

"Serve"

My Obedience is Only To You,

YHWH God of Love,

My One Elohim.

For many men have come in Your Name,

But their words and hearts cause division,

Confusion,

Destruction,

Chaos.

But Not You.

For You Give Peace and Understanding,

Hope and Beauty.

Your Ways are Higher Than mans ways,

So he does not understand the length,

Depth,

Height,

Weight,

In which Your Immeasurable Wisdom is Given.

You have No Box.

You Are Finite,

Yet Infinite.

One and All.

Alpha and Omega.

How can the human mind possibly comprehend?

It cannot,

Therefore,

I Listen To You,

However You "Speak" to Me.

I Dwell With You in The Secret Place,

Which is where I cannot fathom Your Greatness,

But it is Ingrained in The Depths of My Spirit,

My Soul,

My Heart.

I Keep My Heart With You,

Focusing on what is Unseen,

The Everlasting.

I Keep My Mind With You,

Seated Above,

Not with those in the flesh of the earth.

Up Here,

Is where I Hear You,

See You,

Know You.

Where Love is Our Bond,

Which no man shall separate.

"Master Teacher"

What an Honor it is to be Taught One on One with The Master Teacher!

I have often taken this time for granted.

I have felt alone.

I have felt no one understands.

I have been led astray by men and their own motives.

I have been tricked by the adversary.

But all of those things have only brought me Closer to You.

You have Cured my Loneliness,

I Know I'm Never Alone.

You Understand All of Me,

Better than Myself.

You have Placed The Knowing In My Heart,

And anytime man has twisted Your Word,

You have Drawn Me In and Revealed Truth.

You have Revealed the enemy's plans.

And You have Reminded me that Your Plans are the Prosperous Ones,

The Only Ones I Need.

Each time I have Overcome, Only because of You.

How Blessed Am I to be Taught in The Kings Chambers!

What an Honor to have Keys to The Kingdom!

What a Privilege to Meet You In The Upper Room!

No matter how many times the world tries to take me from You,

You are Always Here,

Welcoming Me Back Home,

Cheering Me On,

Drawing Me Nearer and Nearer to You.

I do not take you for granted,

My King,

I Seek Your Wise Counsel Only You can Give,

And I will Continue On this Pursuit With You,

Heaven Bound.

"Grace and Wisdom"

Your Grace and Wisdom Surround Me,

Like a Soft Serenade that Whispers Sweetly to My Heart,

My Soul.

It Tenderly Touches My Whole Being,

Causing My Heart to Sing its Joyous Song,

Exuberating Your Holy (Qodesh) Spirit,

Through Song, Dance, Poetry, Romance.

Your Never Ending Grace Overflows My Essence

And Exceeds Out,

Giving Grace to Any and All who accept this Gift You Bestow.

The Life that You have Revived Within me,

Bursts with Passion, Innocence and Adventure,

Like the Child You Remind us to Portray.

My Life, My Being, You have Resurrected.

I Bow in Reverence at All Your Glory.

The Sweetness I have Tasted from Your Words and Wisdom,

Overflows from My Lips like Honey Dripping from the Hive.

In Your Sweet, Warm, Unconditional Love,

Is where I Abide,

Forevermore.

"I AM Rich"

Your Boundless Blessings Pour Upon Me.

I AM Entrenched in the Riches of You,

The Riches of Your Glorious Life and Astounding Love.

I AM Rich Because of You.

I Am Rich in Wisdom,

Because I have Asked, You so Graciously have Given.

I AM Rich in Glory,

That which You have Granted because of Grace.

I AM Rich in Faith,

Because of the Hope that Stays Alive in You.

I AM Rich in Wonder,

Because of All the Beauty You have Shown Me.

I AM Rich in Kindness,

Because You have Shown Me Mercy.

I AM Worthy of these Riches,

Because You have Forgiven Me.

And I AM Forever Grateful for the Rich and Bountiful Blessings You have Bestowed Upon Me!

"Oil of Joy"

The Joy of The Good Lord is My Strength.

Surely Goodness and Mercy shall Follow Me All the Days of My Life.

He has Poured the Oil of Joy Upon Me.

For Joy has Come from within the mourning.

I have Sown in Tears,

And I shall Reap in Joy.

Rejoice!

For the Time has Come to Enjoy in Joy!

His Gladness shall Spring Forth as a Gushing River,

A River of Life,

With a Sweet,

Satisfying Taste of Serenity,

And a Rainbow Bursting Through the Silence,

Flowing from the Tip of My Tongue.

For He has Given My Voice a Song to be Sung!

One that Lights the Soul Ablaze,

That Awakens the Dry Bones,

And Revives the Heart Back to Life!

So Stand Tall,

Sing!

Dance!

Rejoice!

Praise!

For The King has Come!

His Cup of Joy is for All to Partake in,

And His Well Never Runs Dry.

"Holy Spirit"

Come Alive! Come Alive!

Your Holy Spirit Fire Flows through Me,

Reviving Me,

Purifying Me.

As I Rise from the Slumber,

As I Rise to My Feet,

As I Rise and Raise My Hands to You,

You Strengthen Me,

You Fill Me with Your Holy Fire,

Igniting the Fire within My Being,

Within My Heart,

Where the Passion Burns for You.

Reviving my Whole Being,

My Soul Ignited in One with You.

I AM Alive in You.

I have been brought back to Life because of Your Burning,

Unconditional,

Agape Love.

Your Truth hits me to the Core,

And Awakens the dry bones that had been dead.

I was dead.

And I was Revived.

You died and Resurrected,

And in You, Christ,

I have died and been Revived,

Bringing back the Spark,

The Fire of Life.

Living True with You,

In Your Glory, Your Might,

Your Astounding Love that Surrounds Me,

Fills me with Passion, Purpose and Endurance,

So I can Walk Bravely and Mightily in Your Truth and Love.

O Holy, Precious, Almighty One,

You have Raised me back to Life!

"Shine"

Shine!

Shine Your Light Upon The World!

You are a Star,

Born to Rise and Shine.

For I have Given You a Gift,

One which can Only be Received by You.

One which can Only be Given by You.

This Gift is For You to Hold,

Yet also for You to Share.

You must Be The Light I have Shone You to Be.

The Bright Shining Star that You Are,

Is a Masterpiece of which I have Knitted and Woven so Perfectly,

So intricately.

It is You.

You are a Miracle.

You are My Masterpiece.

You are My Shining Star.

You are My Love.

For I Am in You,

And You are in I.

I Ask You,

Darling,

To Shine and Bestow the Gifts that You have been Given.

Present Your Presence as My Own,

For the Present is the Perfect Time to Present the Gift of My Presence Through You.

As I Walk With You,

I AM In You,

And We Shine in Glorious Esteem,

Walking Hand in Hand,

Heart to Heart,

In The Grand Majesty of This Mighty and Precious Love.

"She is...."

She is Tender,

She is Mighty.

She Wears The Crown of Light,

With Wisdom Upon Her Head.

Her Crown is Adorned with the Finest Jewels.

Those of Rubies, Crystals, Sapphire and Emerald.

As Her Light Shines,

So too does Her Crown Sparkle and Shimmer.

She is Clothed with Dignity and Splendor,

A Magnificent, Glorious Sight to Behold.

Her Heart Shines with this same Pristine Beauty.

The Love she Carries Radiates a Thousandfold.

This Beautiful Gift she was Granted by Christ, The Most High,

The Sacred Heart,

Given to Share and Radiate in Hopes that this Love will Touch the Lives of all.

She Honors her Most Prized Treasure,

Her Heart,

That He has Freely Given,

To break the chains of bondage.

And as She Stepped Up and Claimed this Most Cherished Adornment,

He has Gifted Her more Wisdom,

More Support,

More Value in Knowing Her Own Value.

For She had to See that She was The Prize,

And has Been All Along.

Her Heart,

Her Soul,

Was All that was Needed,

To just Surrender it to Him,

And She would be Gifted Life,

And Real,

True Agape Love.

So She Did.

And Now She Stands Firm and Faithful with Him by Her Side,

Every Step of The Way.

She Laughs without fear of the future,

And Rejoices in Times to Come.

Kingdom Come, Kingdom Bound.

"Beauty for Ashes"

You have Mended My Broken Heart,

O Sovereign One,

As Only You Could Do.

You have Purified it and Created a Clean Heart within Me.

You have Opened the Eyes of My Heart to See All of You.

You have Turned My Mourning Into Joy,

O Sovereign One,

As Only You Could Do.

You have Taken the Bottle of Tears,

As I have Poured it Upon Your Feet.

You have Comforted me,

As You have Poured the Oil Upon My Head.

You have Taken and Lifted this Heaviness,

O Sovereign One,

As Only You Could Do.

You Lifted My Hands, as I Lifted My Eyes to You,

Sight Set High.

You Gave Me Breath,

Gave Me Life to Raise My Voice in Song to You.

You have Never Forsaken Me,

O Sovereign One,

You have Turned My ashes Into Beauty.

You have Clothed Me in Your White Robe of Righteousness.

You have Adorned Me in Your Finest Jewels.

You have Crowned Me in The Light,

And I Shine Brightly,

For Your Glory.

Wisdom

"Wisdom Speaks"

Connect with Me, says Wisdom.

I will Guide You to the Place of All the Answers.

This Place is Unknown.

You must Trust, that what I Reveal to You,

Is for You.

You must Follow My Voice,

Hear My Subtle Whispers that Speak to Your Soul,

That Penetrate Your Being,

That Show You Truth.

My Revelations may not always make sense at the Time,

But they will be Understood when they are Meant To Be.

I may not Present Myself in a manner that your ears understand,

But I will Touch the Deepest Parts of You.

I will Call You,

And Give You My Teachings,

When you Are Ready.

I will Teach You when to be Silent,

And when to Speak.

I will Teach You when to Listen,

And when to Move.

You will Know My Voice.

Others will Know My Voice too,

As You Speak My Words.

I will be Known by The Wise,

And the Faint alike,

For My Presence Echoes to Any and All who Need Me.

It cannot be shut out.

When I AM Present,

I AM Known.

I AM Heard.

I AM Felt.

I AM the Soil,

I AM the Seed,

I AM the Sprout,

I AM the Sapling,

I AM the Tree.

I AM All of these,

Yet I Take Time to Grow,

And I AM Present with those who Need Me in each Stage of My Existence.

No Less, No More.

I AM the Larvae,

I AM the Caterpiller,

I AM the Cacoon,

I AM the Chrysalis,

I AM the Yoke,

I AM the Butterfly.

I AM Growth.

I AM Transformation.

I Bring Nectar for Your Tongue,

And Vision to Your Eyes.

I AM a Valued Treasure,

And once You have Found Me,

I will Show You Wonders.

I will Show You Truth.

For without Me, You would stay a seed.

Without Me, You would be lost in the dark.

I Thrive In Light, In Life, In Love.

I AM Right Here,

Inside of You,

You just have to See Me.

"Who Are You?"

I AM Open to Receive You.

Show me who You are.

I See You, I AM You.

I See You in the Misty Morning Dew,

In the Sun Rising over the Water, behind the Mountain.

I See You in the Evening with the going down the same.

I See You in the Twinkling of the Stars,

And in the Light and Dark of the Moon.

I See You in the Blossoming of the Spring Flower,

And in the Withering of the Autumn Trees.

I See You in the Eyes of a Child,

And in the Eyes of My Own.

I See You Everywhere, and Oh how Magnificently,

Wonderfully,

Beautiful, You Are.

"Your Majesty"

I Bow Down and Look Up to Your Majesty.

The Beauty that Surrounds Me Takes My Breath Away,

And Restores My Breath With Life.

You Send Your Heavenly Guides,

Speaking with Me Through Your Creation.

I See the Rarity of the Luna Moth,

I See the Work of the Bees,

I Hear the Song of the Cardinal,

I Hear the Call of the Eagle,

I Follow the Slow and Steady Turtle.

You Show Me In the Waves of the Sea,

The Colors of the Wind,

The Flourishing of a Flower,

The Embers of a Fire,

The Alignment of the Stars.

I See You.

I Hear You.

You are All Around Me,

Surrounding Me In Your Loveliness.

I AM Marveled at Your Majesty.

I AM Glorified at Your Glory.

I AM Amazed at Your Awesomeness.

I AM Exuberant at Your Excellence.

I AM Humbled and Honored to Be a Part of Your Grand Design!

"In the Hidden Kingdom"

You have Opened My Eyes to The Light,

The Truth.

You have Given Me Clear Vision so I can See The Way,

And See what's To Come.

I once was blind,

But Now I See.

You have Handed Over The Keys to The Hidden Kingdom,

Where there are Many Mysteries and Stories.

Mysteries that can Never Be Solved,

And Stories that have No Ending.

Yet they Speak to Me Right Here and Now,

As if You have Planned it All Along.

Because You Have.

You have Planned it From The Beginning,

Yet You Orchestrate it in this Right Now Moment.

What a Grand Symphony You Conduct!

Always Right On Time,

Perfectly In Tune!

What a Captivating Story You Tell!

Leaving me In Wonder and Awe,

Never Knowing The Next Chapter!

What a Marvelous Mystery You Are!

Taking me Into The Great Unknown,

Gathering The Puzzle Pieces Along The Way.

In The Hidden Kingdom,

You Grant Access to The Wisdom of The Ages,

From Age to Age it Renews.

What a Fantastical Door You have Opened,

Which No Man Can Shut,

For his eyes are blind,

And to him there is no door.

But You,

Christ Yeshua,

My Teacher,

My Friend,

King of Kings,

You have Restored My Sight,

You have Shone Me Inside!

"Soaking In the Secret Place"

I Soar High Above and Beyond with You.

You take me outside this Space and Time,

And Into the Secret Place where we reside in Harmony and Peace.

Where Love Flows and has No Bounds.

A place where Eternal Waters Flow,

Glistening with Pristine Beauty,

Cleansing,

Renewing My Mind, Body, Spirit, and Soul.

A place where you Replenish and Refresh My Spirit,

Ceasing it from running dry.

For You are The River of Life,

And in Your Place of Refuge I AM washed Anew,

Refueled and Refilled,

My Cup Runneth Over as You Pour Your Tender Love into My Being,

And Anoint My Head with Oil.

For Here The Light Doth Shine,

For without You My Lamp would be darkened,

My Light would be dimmed.

But You, O Love,

You have awakened My Heart and Soul,

You, My God,

Have shown me The Truth, The Life, Light, and The Way.

You have brought me Into The Secret Place and Shone me just how Glorious a Place it is to Be One with You.

May We Soar Forevermore in this Sacred Conjoining, Converging as One.

"I AM"

I Am Holy and Complete In You.

I Reclaim the Power You have Given Me,

The Power of Love.

The Power of The Great I AM.

For I Walk Boldly in this Power Only You could Bestow.

The Power that Withstands Any and All Things.

The Power that Sets a Fire Ablaze My Being.

The Power that Strengthens and Purifies Me,

All in the Power that Is You,

That Is The Great I AM.

You are My Rock,

My Shield,

My Refuge,

My Covering,

My Secret Place,

My One,

And I AM One With You.

The Power of Love Conquers All,

And My Fortress,

My Kingdom,

Is With You in that Power of Love,

In The Great I AM.

As I Trust in All of You,

Your Glory,

Your Mercy,

Your Majesty,

Your Strength,

Your Guard,

Your Forgiveness,

Your Truth,

Your Unconditional Love,

I too AM that,

I AM.

"Heavenly Mother"

Your Love is so Pure,

So Nurturing.

You keep me Warm and Safe in the Comfort of Your Bosom,

Your Heart.

You Hold Me so Close and Bring Peace to My Being.

You are My Peace.

Queen of Peace.

Lady of Angels.

Lady Amongst The Stars.

You Feed Me Sweetness of Milk and Honey.

Nourishing,

Nurturing.

You Dress me Royally in Rubies and Pearls,

Pure,

Wise.

Heavenly Mother I Adore You.

I Cherish You.

I Honor You.

You Bring Sustenance.

You Show Innocence and Grace,

So Gently and Kindly.

You are The Container,

You Hold The Space.

You are Free Flowing,

Like the Gently Rolling Creek.

Your Heart is Soft and Meek,

Strong and Courageous.

You Shine like The Stars from Heaven Above.

I AM One with You,

Here,

In This Sacred, Immaculate Heart,

In the Warmth of Your Bosom.

"The Angels"

Oh The Angels,

My Heavenly Kin.

How You Teach Me to Be,

Like a Child again.

Dancing and Singing Our Heavenly Tunes.

We Laugh and We Play and Fly Through The Skies,

Making Rainbows, Riding Unicorns, Sailing So High!

Your Sweet Serenade Harmoniously Beats with My Heart.

You Treat me like Royalty,

So Gentle, Kind, Nurturing, Giving,

Yet such a Wise, Strong and Faithful Counsel.

I Love You and Miss You so Dearly,

Yet I know if I Reach Inside,

To Innocence,

Inside this Young Heart,

There You Are,

We Are,

Ready to Play, Dance, Sing Our Harmonious Tune!

"Like The Dove"

Like The Dove,

You Bring Shalom (Peace) Upon My Soul.

You Settle My Mind.

Where there are troubled waters,

That seem as though a mighty storm brews,

Ready to wipe out all in its path,

I Come Back to You,

And We Build a Bridge Over Troubled Waters.

My Thoughts Become as a Steady Flow,

With Your Sweet Serenity Drifting Me Harmoniously With You and All that Is.

You Calm the Storm and Bestow a Peace Upon Me,

One that Surpasses All Understanding.

As You Bring this Peace,

Comfort,

Warmth,

You Brighten My Day,

Bringing a Colorful Rainbow,

Shining its Rays Upon My Being.

Transforming the dark of the storm, into that Translucence of Rainbow Light,

And Into One Bright Light of Your Unconditional Love.

As The Dove Calms the tidal waves of the mind,

So too does She Dance with The Rainbow,

Embracing the Holiness,

Harmony,

Purity,

Love of The Father,

The Mother,

The Child,

Of The Cosmos and All that Is.

For All are One.

Shalom.

"For Every Time and Season"

For Everything there is A Time and A Season,

And He has made All Beautiful in Its Time.

There is No Beginning, there is No End,

All just "Is",

In It's Own "Time".

In Our Time of sorrow,

We Cry and He Collects Our Tears,

And In Turn Takes them and Turns them Into Joy.

In Our Time of doubt,

We Wonder and The Mind is Tossed About,

And In Turn He Gives us Security and a Peace that Surpasses All Understanding.

In Our Time of pain,

We Hurt, we Lash Out,

And In Turn His Grace Tells us that By His Stripes We Are Healed.

In Our Time of despair,

We Feel we have Lost Our Way,

And In Turn He Restores Our Hope, Promising He Knows The Plans He has Planned for us.

He Reminds Us that His Ways are Higher Than our ways.

What He Does "Is" Forever,

There is No Adding or Subtracting.

What "Is", "Is",

And has Already Been Done.

It "Is" the Same,

From Beginning to End,

From End to Beginning.

And in this Speck of Eternal Life,

The Speck of Infiniti,

We are Asked to "do" One Thing,

In Any and Every Season,

In Any and Every Space and Time,

That "Is"....

To LIVE IN Everlasting Love

Love

"Love Speaks"

Connect with Me, says Love.

Feel Me Deeply,

Feel Me Fill Your Being,

Your Spirit with My Presence.

You mustn't forget, Dear Child of Mine,

I AM Your Teacher,

I AM Your Healer,

I AM Your Partner,

I AM Your Joy,

I AM Your Laughter,

I AM Your Innocence,

I AM Your Maker.

I AM the Sweet Serenity You Long For.

I AM the Place You Call Home.

I AM Your Ultimate Truth.

It is Me.

All Me.

I AM Yours,

And You are Mine.

We Are One.

I AM the Great I AM.

Connect with Me, My Love.

I AM never away from You,

I AM Always Right Here with You.

I have never forsaken or abandoned You,

You See,

For I Never Fail.

Love Never Fails.

I do not boast,

I do not envy,

I do not deny,

I do not perish.

I AM Everlasting.

I AM Your Breath.

I AM Your Life.

Come, Follow Me.

Be Strong In Me.

Have Faith In Me.

Have Hope In Me.

Have Life In Me.

I Only Long to Be with You,

And You with I.

Trust Me.

Believe Me.

Open to Receive Me.

I will not forsake You, Dear One.

I Love You with the most Pure Love Imaginable,

Attainable,

Achievable.

When I Look at You,

I Only Know You as My Precious Creation,

A Perfect Image of Me,

The Great I AM.

We Are One,

I have never left you,

I have Always been right there Within You,

Above You,

Beside You,

Ahead of You.

Follow Me, My Love,

My Child,

I will never forsake You,

I will Only Keep You Preciously,

Tightly,

Under My Wings,

Inside My Warmth.

You are Safe with Me.

I AM Right Here,

Always with You,

Connect with Me,

Feel My Presence,

Embrace Me,

For You are All I Long For,

For Now and All Eternity,

We Are Everlasting,

You and I,

We Are One.

One Mind,

One Being,

One Essence,

One Spirit,

One Love.

"One Flame of Eternal Love"

Who AM I, but a Twinkle in Your Eye?

The Great Unknown, yet Feels like Home.

You Take me Deep,

Deeper than the Oceans Floor,

My Heart melts in Pieces,

Down to My Core.

I rest in Your Embrace,

Your Soft,

Sweet,

Joyous,

Miraculous,

Comfortable,

Warm Serenity.

You Surround Me in a Presence I cannot define in words.

It's just a Feeling, A Presence.

One that I cannot escape, and don't wish to.

If I could Lay With You All of My Days,

I would Be Happy.

I would Be Free.

I would Be Perfect.

I would Drown In Your Loveliness,

Your Awe,

Your Perfection.

And I'm okay with that.

Because I AM You, and You are Me.

We Are One.

My God,

My Creator,

The Love of My Life,

You Hold Me like no other can,

And the Taste of Your Love,

The Embrace of Your Love,

Is More Than any man can fathom,

For he does not know how Wonderful,

Marvelous,

Miraculous,

Full You Are.

But I Pray he does.

And if he does,

Than I AM In Love with him too,

As I Know You are Within Him,

As You are Within Me.

How can I put into words this Tender,

Yet Mighty feeling inside of me?

Pure,

Yet Fierce.

I only Pray for mankind to Know You,

To See You,

To Experience You,

To FEEL You.

What he does not know is that it is Already There,

Within Him.

He just has to Find It.

It is There.

Here.

The Best Treasure of All.

Your Love,

My Love,

Our Love,

As the One Love that We Are.

Eternal Love,

Never broken,

Never gone,

Never separated from You.

It will Remain Through All Space and Time.

Through Infiniti.

The Eternal Heart Fire,

The Eternal Flame of Sacred Love,

Of Oneness.

This Flame is but an Eternal Bond between You and I,

But is not separate from You and I,

Because We Are the One Flame,

Burning Passionately,

Yet Flowing Gently,

Easily,

Freely.

My Love For You Will Never Fade.

Your Love For Me Will Never Fade.

This Love, is All We Are.

"Passion of the Sacred Heart"

You Sparked a Fire Within Me!

You set My Heart Ablaze!

The Passion Ignited Within My Whole Being Unquenchably Thirsts for the Purity of Your Flowing River of Life.

The Blazing, Burning of this Sacred Heart Fire Flows in Tandem Serenely with the Tranquil Waters and Engulfs my Physical and Spiritual Essence.

This Mighty Love is Fierce,

Entrenching me with an Aliveness I've never felt before.

Yet this Mighty Love is Pure,

Surrounding me with a Peace that Surpasses all Understanding.

It is a Beautiful Balance of Your Extraordinary Strength,

And Your Gracious Compassion.

It is The Essence, The Being, The Power,

Of The Sacred, Immaculate Heart,

And it Is Yours.

"Song of The Sacred Heart"

You have Restored the Song of My Heart.

I Sing Joyously to the Tune of Our Harmonious Heartbeat.

Where I once was numb,

You Revived me.

Where I once felt pain,

You Healed me.

You have taken my broken Heart,

And Restored and Rekindled its Vitality and Passion.

You have taken my broken Spirit,

And Raised and Reassembled its Life and Holiness.

You have Gifted me a New Song.

One of Power and Strength that comes from You,

O Holy One.

It Flows from My Lips,

Singing and Praising Your Greatness and Unwavering Love.

These Songs You have Blessed me with fill My Soul,

My Heart,

My Body with You,

Holy Spirit,

And Touch the Soul,

Heart,

and Body,

Of All those who are Tuned Into this Magnificent Melody,

Resonating with the Frequency on One Accord,

One Sound,

One Mind,

One Body,

One Love,

Of Christs Sacred Heart,

The Eternal Flame.

"O Sweet Song"

The Serendipitous Symphony of Your Grandoise Love,

Can only be Heard with the Rhythm of my Attuned Soul with Your Magnificent Presence.

You Speak Deeply with the Harmonization of my Mind, Body and Soul,

All in the Holy Place of your Glorious Oneness.

The Melodies of My Being are Engulfed in and around the Melodies of your All Encompassing Grand Goodness.

I Feel Your Presence in and around me.

I Hear Your Words written on My Heart and Soul.

I See Your Miracles playing out before my Eyes.

I Touch Your Creation in Everyone and Everything.

I Taste Your Nectar as Wisdom reaches my lips.

Your Song is One I Remember,

Time and Time again.

It's One I will not forget.

It Transcends All Things.

It is Heard On Time, Everytime.

As You Play on My Heartstrings,

I AM Forever in this Holy Place with You.

You are My Home,

My Peace,

My Joy.

I will not forsake You, Oh Sweet Song.

"Dance of the Divine Orchesrtra"

I AM Woven into the Tapestry of Your Divine Orchestra.

A Dance that Perplexes my mind,

One I cannot fathom in this earthly realm.

But My Being Understands,

Innerstands,

Resonates,

Penetrates,

And Dances Along to a Tune that Our One Heart Shares.

I Delight in this Dance,

As Our Heartsrings Strum in Accordance with this Harmonious Flow.

I Delight in the Sound,

The Sound that Sings to My Soul as You Whisper Sweet Serenades,

Softly in My Ear.

I Delight in the Sight,

As My Eyes are Fixed Upon Your Shining Face,

And I SEE the Depth of You.

As We Dance in Your Divine Orchestra,

I AM Taken Away by Your Heavenly Gaze,

Sent to a Heavenly Place,

Where We Float Amongst the Clouds and Beyond,

With a Choir of Angels,

In the Light of this Magnificent Love.

How Grand a Place to BE.

"Love is In The Air"

Love is In The Air,

Can You Feel it All Around?

Like a Fluffy Cloud Embracing Us In Heavens Bliss.

We Soar In The Sky,

The Son Shining Upon Us,

Keeping Us Warm,

Safe and Protected In All His Shekinah Glory.

He is Our Guardian,

Keeping Us Close and Tight,

As We Weave,

Wax and Wane,

Wings Spread Wide.

We do not grow weary in Well Doing,

No,

For He Keeps Us Fed and Watered.

His Rainbow Gleans In The Sky,

Leading Our Way.

On the darker nights,

The Stars Shine Bright,

Leading Us To The Light of a New Dawn.

Love Is In The Air,

Everywhere We Turn,

For Air is Our Breath,

And I AM Alive because of His Breath of Eternal Life,

And Everlasting Love.

"Fragrance of Your Love"

Like The Rose,

You Bring Passion and Romance to My Life.

Your Eternal Love Sparks the Flames of My Sacred Heart Fire,

And Entrenches My Being with Our Melodious Song,

Everlasting throughout the ages,

Reminding me of Our Royal Heritage,

As We Dance to the Rhythm of Our Heartbeat.

Like The Honeysuckle,

You Bring Sweetness and Wisdom to My Life.

Your Eternal Love Tastes like Honey,

Overflowing from Your Lips, to Mine,

Seeking Your Word,

Speaking Your Words,

As the River of Life Flows from Your Essence,

Through My Being,

As Your Words Become Mine to Live By.

Like The Lilly,

You Bring Purity and Virtue to My Life.

Your Eternal Love Washes Away all the Impurities of My Mind, Body and Soul,

Revitalizing My Spirit,

Raising Me,

Renewing Me,

Sanctified and Set Apart.

Like The Magnolia,

You Bring Beauty and Endurance to My Life.

Your Eternal Love Shows me the Miraculous Wonders right before My Eyes,

Proving Your Steadfast Love for Me,

And, In Time, after Traveling through the Great Unknown with You,

Revealing Your Works through the trying of Faith,

Confirming how Grace Paves the Path to Righteousness.

Like The Sunflower,

You Bring Light and Joy to My Life.

Your Eternal Love Shines a Light in the darkness,

Like the Stars Twinkling Bright, on a Full Moon Night,

And with the Dawn, bringing a Fresh Burst of Sunshine for me to wake to with each New Day,

Seeing All Your Majesty with the Eyes of Innocence, Wonder and Awe.

Like all these Flowers,

Your Sweet Fragrance of Eternal Love brings an Abundance of Blessings,

And Fills My Surroundings with Eternal Bliss and Eternal Life.

"Your Transcendental Love"

Your Love Exudes me.

I AM so Thankful to experience a Love such as this.

The Deepest, Most Pure Love Imaginable.

The Depth of Your Love cannot be described,

Only Felt with every Fiber,

Depth,

Breath,

Of my Whole Being.

You Transcend the mind,

Open My Heart to All Possibilities.

Tranquil as The Dove,

Serene as the Sparkling Oasis,

Yet Fiery like the ruins of a great Forest Fire,

Engulfing all in its Path.

The Strength and Conviction of Your Love is like the Mightiest Oak Tree,

Willow Tree.

A Steady Solid Rock of a Firm Foundation.

It Withstands and Holds True through Any storm.

And the Beauty of it All?

Your Love,

This Mighty Love,

Is My Love.

For You are Within Me.

How Blessed and Grandiose as to Know that I AM that Love that You are!

You have Shown me Love that can Only be Shown by You, Almighty One.

My Soul is the Essence of You,

Oh Great, Holy Creator,

And Oh what a Wonderful,

Breathtaking,

Serene,

Warm,

Soft,

Firm,

Sweet,

Embrace it is.

Thank You,

For I have Come to Know You,

Face to Face,

Eye to Eye,

Heart to Heart,

Soul to Soul.

"Give to Thee"

I Pour Out My Love to Thee,

I Give Thee All of Me.

Flesh and Bone,

Mind and Soul.

For In You is Life,

There is no death,

You Have My Heart,

You Have My Breath.

Eternal Love is All that's Real,

Eternal Life Marks The Seal.

I AM One,

One In You,

One In Love,

A Love So True.

The Truth Is Here,

It Makes Us Free,

Once being blind,

Now We See.

Seeing The Light,

Lighting The Way,

Forevermore,

Here We Stay.

Home

"Set Apart Love"

My Love for You is Set Apart,

Nothing can compare.

You know just the Right Way to Revive My Hope,

Restore My Youth,

Replenish My Spirit.

The Way You Speak to Me is like Music to My Ears.

The Way I Speak to You is like Honey Flowing from My Lips.

I Cherish Our Conversations.

It's like I Know You More and More,

Deeper and Deeper,

And I feel Warm in that Embrace.

Like You Know Every Piece of Me.

You See Me,

You Hear Me,

You Comfort Me.

My Soul Rests in Your Sweet Embrace,

Holding Me so Firmly, Yet so Gently,

Letting me Know You are Always Here with Me,

Never Forsaking Me.

I Trust in Your Love,

In This Love,

In Our Love.

I Trust where it Leads Me and Guides Me,

The Truth, The Way, The Light, Life.

It is My True Compass,

Always Leading Me Home.

If ever I go astray,

You never leave My Side,

You are Always with Me,

Unto The End,

End to Beginning,

Where We Meet Again.

Right Here,

Right Now,

Where My Soul can Rest.

Where I AM at Peace.

You are My Peace,

My Comfort,

My Refuge,

My Strength,

My Grace,

My Purity.

You are My Everything.

You are My Home.

I will Always Return to You.

"No Greater Love"

You have Sacrificed Yourself for me.

You have Continued to have Mercy on me,

Grace with me,

Patience for me.

You Chose to Lay Down Your Life,

For me.

You Love me that Much.

So Much So that You Never Gave Up.

You Never Have and You Never Will.

You Endured So Much Pain for me.

So Much Hurt,

Sorrow,

Persecution,

So Much Pain!

You Faced it All,

Just for me!

It wasn't in vain.

I Feel Your Love.

I Feel You.

I'm so Thankful for You.

You Gave Me Life,

There is No Greater Love!

Letter of Faith

This Journey With You takes Much Faith.
It takes Much Trust.
It takes Much Surrender.
It's like walking off a cliff,
Or like walking on water.
To totally Let Go and Surrender All to You,
To Believe You Will Take Care of it All,
Is what defines "Walk by Faith, not by sight".
It takes time to Build the Trust it requires for one to Walk one day at a time,
One Step at a time.
But if I Follow Your Steps,
And take You for Your Word,
I Know that All Good Things are Here,
And From You,
And that You Always Provide.
For You Provide for the birds,
For the lilies,
So how much more shall You Provide for I?
You Know what I Need,
And so long as I Follow You,
I shall worry naught.
Thank You,
For Always Taking Care of me,
And never forsaking me.
Love,
Your Daughter, Your Friend, Your Love

It is a Tale as Old as Time,
A Song as Old as Rhyme.
Like Fine Wine it is Preserved,
And Well Refined.
From Genesis to Revelation,
Its Story is Told Time and Time Again,
From Beginning to End,
End to Beginning,
It Is Continual.
The Redeeming of The Times,
And Times Past.
Dying and Being Reborn,
Labouring and Delivering.
When We Seek and Find Truth,
When We Find We Are One,
The One Truth that Lights The Way,
Through All Space and Time,
Throughout The Ages,
It Never Changes.
That is When We Come to The Point of No Return,
Because there is No Where to Return To.
The Only Way is Up and Out,
In and Through.
The Kingdom is Here,
And Unto Days of Old and New,
Everlasting Love Is The Key!

Made in the USA
Monee, IL
17 October 2024